10/22/21
Jeanam - S
my life. Ble
Be well, Be love, Be peace —
we do go back a few years,
Love + prayers, Carol

LOVE NOTES FOR THE JOURNEY—

POETIC GEMS TO LIGHT(EN) YOUR SPIRITUAL PATH

JACKIE COMPTON

This book is lovingly dedicated to

John Bartlow

my wonderful friend of 51 years,
the first person who recognized my writing ability
and encouraged me to dream.

Thank You, My Dear Friend.

About the Author

Jackie Compton is the author of this newest poetic work *Love Notes for the Journey—Poetic Gems to Light(en) Your Spiritual Path.* This little book is packed with inspirational poems that will help light your path and lighten your load.

Jackie's past writing experiences include secular articles in magazines and blog posts, poems in various anthologies, and two chapters in a medical textbook. She first began writing about the things of the spirit at 10 years of age. Around that time she became aware of the power of healing energy, later becoming a massage therapist and Reiki Master. Jackie currently uses Reiki and Quantum Touch in an energy healing practice.

To Jackie, life is an adventure. Life has offered Jackie experiences of pain, integration and healing. After suffering with severe depression and addiction, Jackie learned the need for, and the gifts of, self-reflection, intuition, and vulnerability for spiritual and emotional growth.

The simple words in this book offer you, Dear Reader, the assurance that you are not alone. It takes great courage to look, see and uplift one's consciousness. The Universe conspires to help us. As we walk our journey, we meet up with like-minded others. The moment we say "Yes" and step onto the path, the energy around us stirs and invisibly supports and feeds us. Life always provides what we need, when we need it.

If you are beginning to dabble in spiritual things, these poems will inform you of the joy that awaits your further exploration. If you are struggling along your path, these poems will give you hope. And if you are basking in Life's glow, these poems will celebrate with you the feeling of serenity and bliss.

So, Dear Reader, may the words in this book sooth you, inspire you, encourage you, and challenge you to seek the deeper part of You. May these words light your path and lighten your load, and may you find peace, joy, purpose and love on your journey.

Table of Contents

Ode to a Friend......................................1

Praying for Someone........................2

Egg White or Meringue 3

Chasing the Dog...............................4

To the Degree....................................5

A Budding Flower.............................6

Butterfly Prayers 7

Always From the Inside Out.............8

Christ as Bread.................................9

Crying Tears of Joy.........................10

Easter..11

Energy Healers................................12

Entrustment.....................................13

Frontliners 14

Gemstones..15

Giving 18

React or Respond? 19

Giving Others Hope and Love 21

Juneteeth 22

Love Speaks.....................................23

May Each Step You Take Today 24

Memorial Day 25

Mining Gold...26

My Boomerang 29

My Drum..30

Nebulousness of Love...32

The Pandemic...34

Precious Girl 36

The Red Rose and the Yellow Tulip............................37

Revel in the Ocean of Divine Water 39

The Eagle and the Forest...40

Self-Forgiveness 42

Share Your Heart Wherever You Go............................43

Strangers 44

Tao of Water 45

The Caterpillar 47

The Dance 48

A Place Only the Wise Know 49

The 43 Year Flood 53

The Stallion and the Eagle 55

The Light That Beckons...57

The Maker and the Made 58

The Mother Harpist...60

The Power of a Nurse 62

Out of the Dark 64

The Power of "I Am"...68

The Soaring of Powerful Eagle 70

The Violin 72

The Way of It 73

Those Who Love Selflessly 76

We Are All Teachers 78

When All Else Fails 79

Your Prayer Creates Your Life 80

Centering Prayer 81

Faith is Believing and Knowing 82

Castles in the Air 83

Knowing the Absolute Truth 86

Stepping Into the Waters of Life 87

Spirit Provides Our Need 88

A Limerick About Job (from the Bible) 89

The Oasis 91

Circle of Life 92

Love is Like the Dazzling Sun 93

Prodigal 94

Three Little Words 96

Throwing Stones 97

Father's Day 98

Wisdom 100

The Miracle 104

Ode to a Friend

You looked into my eyes and gently said, "Tell me."
Your tenderness invited me into a safe, sacred space,
I cried every time we met, each time revealing
more and more fear, anger and shame hidden a lifetime.

You gave me hope that someday my tears would stop,
you honored my sadness with a tear of your own,
you encouraged me to confront my inner night,
by shedding light into my soul to reveal hope.

You applauded me when I said "No."
And though there were times when you felt inadequate
and floundered over what to say next,
you always said the right thing
because God sat between us.

What you did was precious indeed.
You saw the Divine Powerful of me
and you beckoned me to love and claim
the Magnificence that I AM.

Praying for Someone

Praying for someone is
the most sacred commitment
that a person can offer up
on behalf of another person.

Praying is the placing of that person
into the safekeeping of something
higher or greater than themselves
with the hope and belief
that healing can come to the person.

Praying is faith in action.

Praying is the giving over of one's own
hopes, thoughts, fears and powerlessness
to this higher power, not knowing the outcome,
usually during a time of vulnerability or harm.

Praying is love in action.

Praying unleashes the
most powerful energy in the universe—Love,
And Love can heal every hurt.

Praying is stewardship in action.

Praying advocates for the person,
invites the person, encourages them
to re-member to the Life Force
and to re-mind them
of who they really Are.

Of all the gifts we can give to another,
praying for them is the greatest gift of all.

Egg White or Meringue

Egg white, with its slimy, gelatinous, evasive,
primordial consistency, is not pleasant.
Whipping egg white transforms the slimy, ugly goo
into magnificent towering peaks
of heavenly meringue pleasure.

Sometimes we are lowly, ugly, difficult
and unpleasant to be around,
but when touched by a power greater than ourselves,
we are transformed into an expansive,
beautiful, pleasant being.

The egg white and meringue are the same substance,
just in a different form.
What form do I want to take today?
Egg white or meringue?

Chasing the Dog

"You damn dog! Gracie, come here!
I don't have time for this today!"
I glance at my watch. "Shit."
Gracie taunts me again to react.

I chase her and she runs—
runs, it seems, with purpose,
as if wanting to lead me somewhere—
to an ecstatic place she knows well,
but I am lost to.
I sit down, frustrated with the futility of the pursuit.

Just out of reach, Gracie wags her tail eagerly,
poised to cavort at my next lunge.
I stay still. Soon her tail stops wagging,
she cocks her head, jumps in my lap and licks my face.

Life is frustrating when we chase elusive imps
like money, lust, approval and things.
When we allow ourselves to let loose of control,
then heaven blesses us with the joy
of the timeless moment.
Sitting and waiting quietly in the Kingdom
brings Grace, which nuzzles us with love and peace.

To the Degree

We can be free, to the degree
that we have unshackled ourselves
from our fears and false, limiting beliefs.

We can accept others, to the degree
that we are comfortable
with our own humanness.

We can love God and others, to the degree
that we can embrace God's gifts for us
and share those gifts with others.

Each day, to the degree that we can
celebrate ourselves and others by
choosing love over fear, we are free.

A Budding Flower

The bulb lies dormant beneath winter's snow,
but then slowly roots emerge and
web themselves deep into the soil,
feeding from earth's nourishment.

Then upward it grows through the dirt,
unhesitating, undaunted, bending itself
around obstacles of rock, dirt and roots,
yearning for the sun and air.

The stalk emerges from the earth
and green leaves form, then the pedals
open slowly to the warming sun,
which invites it to bloom
and adorn its surroundings.
And people come to study its grace,
to drink in its beauty and simplicity,
to smell its sweet fragrance,
and to feel one with God through it.

You are the budding flower, my friend.
You have emerged from the cold and dark
and have planted your roots in God's nourishment.
Then you started to grow spiritually,
facing each challenge that came upon your path.
And now your pedals are opening
and you can feel God's warmth pressing upon you
in your dedication to Truth,
as you drink in the meaning of Love.

People seek out your simplicity and beauty,
and come away with a peaceful heart
from having spent time
with one of God's glorious creations.

Butterfly Prayers

Offer your prayers,
not as a task pushing
a stone up a hill,
but as a pleasure
resting as a butterfly
upon a child's finger.

And your butterfly beauty will bless
all those it lands on
and who view it
from afar.

Always From the Inside Out

always from the inside out
healing is from inside out
heat, radiating from
the center to the perimeter
circling, changing, giving

touching from the heart
intertwining like musical tones
singing a melody of life
giving to each other and
receiving from giving

our Heavenly Home within us
the small inner voice of Soul
the center from which we grow
we sing our song of transition
a healing for ourselves and others

and in being raised from our darker self
we reach for a hand
that intertwines with our own
and from the inside out
always from the inside out

love, peace, acceptance
circling, changing, giving
we sing in harmony with gratitude
as we help others heal
always from the inside out

Christ as Bread

The luscious, tantalizing aroma of homemade,
hand-kneaded baked bread,
the enticing warmth of its touch,
and its texture-rounded shape
stimulate a deep need in us.
Bread nourishes our physical body—
Christ nourishes our spiritual body
and stimulates the deepest need in us to be One.

A shy person who was afraid to talk to people
joined the church welcoming committee.
She transformed her fear by making bread
for the newcomers.
The gifting of her bread welcomed seekers
who entered our doors,
and it blessed everyone with an enticing
invitation to communicate, connect and
find peace and friendship with each other in Spirit.

Christ, through that bread, broke through
our friend's fear and self-consciousness—
and Christ, through that bread, filled all
with the universal substance of God's Grace.
Bread symbolizes the Christ essence of us.
Let us become one body by feeding each other
with welcome, community and love.

Crying Tears of Joy

Crying tears of joy is really soul surfing on Lake Ecstasy.

Easter

Jesus and the Easter experience are our renewal pinnacle.
We enter our sanctuary beaten and bloodied,
pained from victimhood, neglect and untruths,
and we wait in our dark cave.

We wait for Light to pierce our darkness, to raise us
from fear to love
from brokenness to wholeness
from separation to oneness.

We patiently rest in God,
waiting to be restored and blessed.
Then, with quiet knowing, we realize …
we *are* Love, we *are* Whole, and we *are* One,
and that we have *always* been Love, Whole and One.

Resting in surrender upon the All Good transforms us from
form to formless,
from concept to presence,
from human to divine.

Our awakening calls others to come forth from their caves
to inherit Love, Joy, Peace and Purpose.
Easter is every day, and it invites us to sit in the stillness,
embrace our Being, and be resurrected as Christ Light.

Energy Healers

Energy healers do not heal, fix or change … anything.
By holding a high vibration
and affirming the client's True Essence,
energy healers create a sacred space for the client
to embrace their own Spiritual Wholeness.
Divine Energy and the client are the true healers.

Entrustment

And the angel said, "Unto you a child is given"

In the deep darkness of the night
there appeared above a beckoning light.
Did everyone see the light so dear?
Or hear the angels sing? Who did hear?

And those seeing, hearing, did they sense danger
while Mary birthed Jesus near the manger?
Or were they excited, happy, and praying?
All the devoted ones anticipating?

Many of us wait years and years
patiently, anxiously, with hope, fears and tears.
It seems love and joy elude us much.
In our stable we wait for God's touch.

We wait in our stable for God to prepare
our hearts and souls for the gift He bears.
The gifts of love, peace, and jubilant joy
at the placement of a little girl or boy.

And then God's Light and the miracle occur
Bringing a gift, not frankincense or myrrh,
but entrustment with the placement of a child—
The heart sings joyously and we smile.

And oh the splendor, when our sweet Lord blesses,
as with a finger, our face He caresses,
and what more precious gift can we receive
than God's new life, we do believe.

Frontliners

Here's a little poem
to you frontliners
Nothing that you're doing
is ever minor.

Eating on the go
there's no rest at the diner
Your dedication to us
there is nothing finer.

Thousands of patients
but of your kind so few
Working day and night
sometimes all the way through.

We could never ask
for anyone more true
We're grateful indeed
for all that you do.

You seem everywhere at once
moving your ass
Serving all with mercy
you are really first class.

We pray in our heart
the pandemic will soon pass
Thank you so much
to you we raise our glass.

Gemstones

Bill was a gemstone
He was silver and gold
But he never was shown it
He never was told.

He grew up believing
Just what he was told
They never did tell him
He was silver and gold.

They really didn't see him
As a spirited guy,
Not knowing he's silver
He was depressed and shy.

He grew into manhood
Not knowing his gold
He was a scared little boy
Frozen and cold.

Mary was a gemstone
She was silver and gold
But she never was shown it
She never was told.

She grew up believing
Just what she was told
They never did tell her
She was silver and gold.

They saw her as different
They didn't ask why
Not knowing she's silver
Alone, she would cry.

She grew to be woman
Not knowing her gold
She felt like a nothing
In a submissive role.

They married each other
Both blind to their gold
"Live for each other"
That's what they were told.

He saw her as mommy
Craving love denied
He felt if he pleased her
Then he'd be able to fly.

She saw him as daddy
Feeling ignored and abused
She felt if she pleased him
She wouldn't be confused.

He saw her as mommy
She saw him as dad
They never did look at
The gold that they had.

She went into counseling
He went into group
Trying to sort out
This big messy goop.

They both had their silver
They both had their gold,
Not knowing it's there
It's hard to behold.

But friends came along
Saw the gold in their hearts
And boldly told them
They could make a new start.

So they opened their fists
Their fingers they spread
And with grateful hearts
They were divinely led.

They did their inner work
Tamed their own mind
Built their own identity
They were no longer blind.

They claimed their own gold
Stopped their internal mayhem
Saw each other's beauty
Each a precious sparkling gem.

They now live in harmony
Spiritually growing and free
Changing their declaration
From "me" to "we."

To love and to listen
To your heart, it's a must
The gold that's inside us
We must believe and trust.

God offers us heaven,
Surrender to His touch
That price may seem daunting
But the blessings are so much.

Giving

I love flowers, and I love giving flowers.
I had a purple rose bush once that was not flowering.
After several weeks, one little bud finally formed,
and I sweet-talked it for a week, encouraging it to grow.
I was elated when one small bud was about to bloom.

Later that day, my four year old daughter came to me,
holding her hand behind her back.
She could barely contain her glee
as she thrust her little hand toward me,
presenting that little purple bud to me as a present.
I stared at the bud and my heart sank.
Then, as if in slow motion, my vision moved
from the bud to my daughter's unfettered beaming smile.

That day I learned that I may not always get what I want,
but life offers infinite bouquets of love
when we can see beyond the small finite.

React or Respond?

My four year old daughter stands in front of me,
presenting me with a purple rose bud
that I had been nursing along for weeks
and which was about to finally open.

Seeing the rose bud and
seeing my daughter's beaming smile,
I could have reacted like my mother did when I was six.
She spanked me when I handed her a gift
of a bouquet of our neighbor's tulips.
Her reacting out of anger, embarrassment and fear
of neighbor judgment left me
with a painful emotional scar toward giving.
That childhood shame flashed through me
as I looked at my daughter and the rose bud.

What do I do? How do I honor her generosity
and uphold her giving nature
but also direct her away from my flowers?
Instead of reacting as my mother did,
I asked for Guidance. An idea flashed.
I knelt down beside her, took the rose bud from her,
and responded.

"It's beautiful. Thank you so much. I love it!"
Her eyes lit and her smile broadened.
"But, you know what, the ones I like the most of all
are the little yellow ones that are all over the lawn.
If you want to make me really happy,
don't pick the roses from now on,
pick the little yellow ones for me."

Her little body undulated with uncompromised joy.
She ran out the door and came back minutes later
with a fistful of 50 yellow dandelions.
I profusely thanked her, placed them in a small vase
and we admired them together.

In every interaction we have,
we can choose to react
out of our fearful ego unconsciousness
or respond out of
our loving Christ consciousness.

Giving Others Hope and Love

Giving
others
HOPE
and
LOVE
empowers
them
to
EMBRACE
the
world.

Juneteeth

As we celebrate the freedom of one color —
All the other colors become free also
For there is only one color —
And that is the color of Love

Love Speaks

When I listen to you breathe
with rhythmic resting as you sleep
in the stillness of the night,
an exhilaration fills my heart.

When I'm in pain,
you wipe away my tears
and hold me tight in your arms.
Your encouragement melts away my distress.

When our eyes meet in a crowded room,
and you send me that impish fun-filled glance
that no one else can see,
it makes me giggle with our secret.

When you touch me
with your hands, and lips, and body
and we intertwine in amorous passion,
my being leaps with rapturous delight.

But mostly,
it is when we are alone together,
silent and serene in each other's presence,
that loves speaks blissful.

May Each Step You Take Today

May each step you take today
leave a trail of love that others will walk on.

Memorial Day

When all of us can put down our defenses
and open ourselves to the Universal Love Force
that weaves us all together in one united flag,
then we will stop killing, not only each other ...
We will stop killing our animals, our land, our air,
our water ... we will stop killing ourselves.

Our greatest tribute to those who have fallen
will be to love ourselves and each other
so we never need to engage in war again.
Finding peace inside ends all wars outside.

Mining Gold

Are you mining for gold outside yourself?
or
Are you mining for gold inside yourself?

It can be difficult and harsh
or
It can be easy and gentle

It can take effort and be painful
or
It can give peace and be healing

It can use heavy equipment
or
It can use light touch

It can be a bone-shaking vibration
or
It can be a cosmic-shaking vibration

It can be physical
or
It can be spiritual

It can be violent
or
It can be blissful

It can be destructive
or
It can be constructive

It can be competitive
or
It can be cooperative

It can be hard
or
It can be soft

It can drill down
or
It can build up

It can extract
or
It can invite in

It can be static
or
It can be dynamic

It can be tangible
or
It can be intangible

It can be greed-oriented
or
It can be abundance-oriented

It can cause separation
or
It can cause oneness

It can be selfish hoarding
or
It can be selfless giving

It can be exclusionary
or
It can be inclusionary

It can be sought by fear
or
It can be sought by love

It can be an outward project
or
It can be an inward journey

Are you mining for gold outside yourself?
or
Are you mining for gold inside yourself?

My Boomerang

My boomerang I toss and it goes around
bringing back what I sent out—up or down
I can send out hate and then I'll frown
or kindness and peace, then love will surround.

Life can be a beach or a stinky armpit
when things go bad, and in pity I sit
I'll love myself and others, and never quit
it's that simple, but difficult I must admit.

Simple's not easy, but it can be done
and when I really do it, it can be fun
when I decide on love, I've already won
soon my woes and blues are on the run.

So I'll hold my head up real high
send good thoughts out into the sky
to that pain I have, I'll wave goodbye
happiness boomerangs, my soul does fly.

My Drum

You are cut from elk and tree,
carrying within you both
the mighty and meek,
the swift and the stationary.

In the cold your sound is flat, off key
your skin is soggy and loose,
but when warmed over a fire
and given nourishment of light
you breathe alive.

Your skin tightens to tone
and your voice reverberates,
sharing your strength and majesty
like the oak and elk from
which you were carved,
sharing your essence of earth and animal.

I seek your consolation for my heart,
which is cold and disconnected,
lacking harmony. My fingers vibrate
with your song gift, and you resonate,
warmly blessing my being and lightening
my soul. I breathe alive.

You share your wisdom and wealth
with me, freely as it was given you,
awakening my own inner paradox of
mighty and meek,
movement and stillness,
until my weak, timid murmur
and your pure untouched peace-tones

blend synergetic to an inspired
proclamation, dedicated to
the Mother Spirit that borne us both.

Nebulousness of Love

Life forms from the DNA molecule,
Its silent, twisting energy
  Breathing,
   Moving,
    Creating … all.

Its ethereal, floating, mystical arrangement
dances within us, causing
  Our heartbeat,
   Our laughter,
   Our pain.

Our love is like the DNA, ever expanding
from within itself creating
  More life,
   More love,
    More growth.

  Awakening, sleeping,
   Expanding, shrinking,
   Giving, receiving.

Asking only that it be allowed to exist,
Imploding, exploding,
Reaching, touching,
Revolving, evolving.
Yearning to evolve, to express itself
  As an atom,
   As the universe,
    As God Itself.

Awakening from our sorrow, we connect,
In living and in death,
  Sharing,
    Touching,
      Blessing,

We One with each other
Ever one, ever forever.

All because of the touch of
the Everlasting Love Force
  Which created the DNA,
    Which created us,
      Which created itself as Love.

The Pandemic

Why don't people wear a mask?
Are they just rebelling to the task?
And do homebodies indignantly bask?
Many questions! Why don't we ask?

We bite others' throats, in anger and hate
We do not realize we are creating our fate
Let us come together before it's too late
If we come together, better times await

We don't hear others cry, we hear our own calls
We act in self-interest, and our behavior appalls
We're afraid to hear the truth so we put up walls
We need to come together before humanity falls

Our enemy's not the virus, our enemy's within
It's the crazy thoughts that make us want to win
It's our fear of "not enough" that is our sin
Striving for perfection to impress our kin

Don't struggle to look like a Hollywood star
Or throw your weight around like a crazy czar
It's not healthy to hide your pain and scar
After all, God loves you just the way you are

Life will be nothing like it was before
We need to connect, open a new door
Let us unite, World, and stop this war
No longer pimp and no longer whore

We think power is all, that it's so grand
Where is it getting us? Please take my hand
Let's put away selfishness, make a new plan
We can save our lives and our Motherland

Are you, dear reader, hearing my drum?
Agreeing, resisting, or thinking "hmmmm."
Feeling powerless, angry or a little numb?
Don't be a victim, raise your thumb

You politicians, our lives are at stake
Just what—oh what—what will it take?
For you to grow balls and stop being flakes
Do your job, damn it—it's time to wake

What … How? You ask. What is the key?
There's no future in "me"—only in "we"
Loving each other will make us free
That sounds lovely, don't you agree?

Here's how we'll do it, no need to shove
Look inside to heaven, and we'll see a dove
When we get the message that we are to love
We will feel God's embrace like a warm soft glove

Then we will all realize that we are one
Away from ourselves we will not have to run
With Love upholding we will not need a gun
The world will be a safe place, when we are done

As we speak our truth and there is no dual
The virus will disappear, it was our tool
For us to embrace, and see our inner jewel
And learn our lesson in this Earth-bound school

Survival or Extinction? It's up to me and you
Let's remember at birth what we once knew
That we are a pure gift, through and through
And we can be that again—let's start anew

Precious Girl

Julie, my sparkling precious girl
you always glimmered in my soul,
even my voice would dance at your name,
it was obvious to all and I was unashamed.

How I love you … oh … how I loved you …
your smile made my soul sing,
your touch warmed my heart,
your words gave me hope.

But now, dearest Julie, only your memory remains,
photos in a book, a well-used ball glove,
I can no longer kiss my sparkling girl,
I can only taste tears and feel the ripping of my heart.

I know you always longed to burn like the brightest star
and now you are with our Lord … *The* Brightest Star,
and my tears are droplets of joy for that,
as our Jesus embraces both of us in His shimmering Love.

Thank you, my Sweet, for loving us,
Thank you for being my daughter and friend,
Thank you, dear Jesus, for sending your Light
in the form of Julie, our precious girl.

The Red Rose and the Yellow Tulip

The red rose stands straight and tall
Making love to the human eyes
Reigning as a majestic queen
Almost haughty, it mystifies

The yellow tulip bemoans its look
Appearing spent when in full bloom
No petals symmetrical or worthy of touch
No one admires … its feeling doomed

"If only I could be like you, Red Rose
Envied and loved by all
If only I could be like you, Red Rose
Then I'd stand gorgeous and tall"

"Dear, Yellow Tulip, envy me not
My beauty does not long last
I am gone early on, with the swing of a blade
My shadow only a moment is cast

"But you, Yellow Tulip, have a gift I do not
That is shared for the whole world to enjoy
This gift so innate … you know it not
It's genuine and cannot be destroyed

"Your fragrance, Dear Tulip, wakes memories of old
Comforting humans deep down in their souls
Your scent thrills the spirit, brings them great peace
Through the air your gift travels and rolls

"Over air streams your presence adorns all who breathe
Bringing peace and good will to the millions
My beauty thrills only a few, for a moment
My unlasting gift to civilians

"If I, Dearest Tulip, could touch them like you
My life would surely be whole
I would be beautiful as the sun's sweet kiss
Happy humans … Oh joy! … My goal"

The rose's sadness touched the tulip
Sharing its vulnerability so deep
And then came a vision to the tulip so clear
That it spoke in almost a weep

"Your beauty is a fleeting thing
Here one moment then quickly gone
But it's the love you touch in a human's heart
That joy! You could dwell on

"For anyone who is touched by a gift
of a rose, a kindness, or a friend
Will be changed by that sharing of love forever
It will warm and never end

"So the giving of you, my Dear Red Rose,
A gift from one person to another
Will travel the world like my gift does
Heart to heart, and will not be smothered

"Humans who treasure us, our beauty, our smell
Are just like us, My Rose Dear
Full of splendor, promise and gifts to share
If only they could see it so clear

"So let's be generous in sharing our gifts
As the Master Gardener has given us all
Given everything generously, treasures so full
Let us serve Him with joy when he calls."

Revel in the Ocean of Divine Water

Revel in the Ocean of Divine Water,
and let it sweep you into blissful, joyous retreat.

The Eagle and the Forest

It is easy to be eagle
flying lazily over the treetops
the wind whisking in my eyes,
I sweep and caw and dance in the sky.

But you, forest, motionless,
your roots clinging to earth's clay,
do you weep for my freedom?
Do your branches wave in the wind for
rescue from your silent and paralyzed prison?

How can you know how beautiful you are
with your greens, and reds, and yellows,
your profound peacefulness, how can you see it?
Would you envy if you could see your own beauty?

Woefully, you cannot see your own beauty,
the majesty of your strength,
the serenity and the silence that people
clamor from the cities to dissolve into,
no, you cannot see your perfection
the turning of your seasons,
your growth in ecstasy and magnificence.

And how can you understand my own envy
to watch you wait, still, silently giving,
shading, sheltering, sustaining,
offering yourself vulnerably for the sake of love
to anyone who can bless or destroy your living breath.

We are both divine,
each singing praise to God's reflection,
for in your silence and stillness
and in my caw and soaring,
we are blessings to each other and all.

Self-Forgiveness

He came in and laid supine on the table.
Smiling but armored, a whirlwind of energy encased him.
"What do you wish to accomplish today?" said the listener.
"I want self-forgiveness," he said.

"Let us begin," said the listener,
as she placed her hands under his head.
In the depth of stark quiet, torrents of unspoken cries
came from him, pleading
   "Please see me … hear me … love me."
The warm hands, guided by the Unseen,
invited him to breathe … to be.

His body twitched and relaxed.
Hypnagogia, the place between wake and sleep,
claimed his consciousness, and he drifted into repose.
After a time, he jerked awake, startled by his surroundings.

The listener smiled down at him, her hands on his chest.
He dropped his head back on the table.
Breathing deeply, and with a tear forming, he said,
"I never told anyone this, but … "

And the armor around his heart cracked, the energy cleared,
  and he saw,
    and he heard,
      and he loved …

Share Your Heart Wherever You Go

Share your heart wherever you go
Your heart is within God's heart
and God's heart is within yours!

Strangers

I was taught to be afraid of strangers
Be suspicious
Keep your distance
Don't talk to them
They may not like you
They might hurt you.

So I obeyed
I stayed silent
Didn't smile at them
Purposely glanced away
Uttered a monotone hello if forced to,
I emotionally hurried behind my wall.

But one day I saw the stranger
That I was most afraid of
The one that caused me to shiver
The one I scanned with distrust
 from the corner of my eye
  ... and I saw
   ... to my dismay
    ... my own old, sad, unloved face
     ... in the mirror.

And in my despair, I closed my eyes and prayed
And a flicker of hope sparked in my chest
And I opened my eyes
  ... and I saw
   ... to my elation
    ... my own indwelling perfection
     ... created in the beginning
      ... when the Word was with God.

Tao of Water

The Big Bang
spewed hydrogen and oxygen into the blackness.
Intelligently guided, the two elements combined to become
the cleansing, purifying, sanctifying substance of life.

A little drop of water
has all the same elements as the ocean.
Each drop's expression is unique with unlimited potential.
It can sustain all of life or it can destroy the entire world.

A water droplet in its own time
returns to the waiting ocean.
Becoming one, the little drop splashes into an
upward and expansive hurrah, rising in power and glory,
celebrating its own expression in euphoria and beauty.
Before its surrender, it was falling …
upon connecting with source, it is rising,
filling our universe with
infinite kaleidoscopes of boundless life.

How much we are like that little water droplet.
We are formed from the ethers,
our substance is divine and intelligent.
Becoming aware, we move from darkness
into our unlimited potential.

Once we release that which holds us
in separating suspension,
we realize oneness with the Universal Ocean.
In blissful realization, we rejoice in an upward,
expansive spiritual splash of hurrah.
Opening us wide as we flow
into our unique divine expression,

we are cleansed, purified, and sanctified
as we blend with the
Ocean of Forever Giving and Forgiving.

Water is life—We are Life,
filling, overflowing, creating, sustaining.
May we experience in our own time that we are
the living water in the Divine Well.

The Caterpillar

The caterpillar dreads its cocoon,
its sight is troubled and dark,
for death is eminent.

And though the caterpillar knows it not,
the Life Force that weaves its cocoon
also creates its butterfly wings,
granting it light from its blindness.

But the caterpillar knows it not
as it weaves its cocoon.
It only knows that the dreaded darkness
that surrounds it is the finishing of a life.
Yet it weaves its cocoon with a loyalty to
Something Greater than itself,
and the Intelligence within its being
unfolds its beauty and freedom.

And in the caterpillar's endeavor
to live its truth, though it be painful,
an essential nuance is added
to the harmony of Life
by its persistence and faith,
and all who see the butterfly
are in awe of its beauty and grace.

Singing our truth, though it be painful,
transforms us from earth-bound caterpillars
to free-floating butterflies.
And Life's longing to be free is complete.

The Dance

We, as parents, engage in an
intricate dance with our children.
We offer our experience, strength and hope to them,
and they innocently offer to us a mirror
to see ourselves in them—
unknowingly inviting us to grow along with them.

We struggle to embrace our dark side
so our light can shine on them.
Sometimes our dance is fluid and gorgeous,
sometimes we trip and step on toes.

If we allow Love to lead the way,
we dance on with our children
creating this magnificent, living expression.
We all find our "voices" and sing as we dance.

A Place Only the Wise Know

There is a place only the wise know.
It is where man is stripped of illusion.

The man sees his Shadow loom over
his head like a hovering curse.
He slaves through work and play,
eluding his Shadow, playing games
to please his merciless, mirrored god.

He dances a mournful waltz,
stepping to other people's tunes,
all the while dripping sweat
in futile endeavor.

He hates every minute of it,
but feels obliged to carry on.
He secretly pleads a
child's naive prayer,
hoping for escape,
perhaps just mercy,
but gets no answer.

Man slaves, games, and dances
even faster, exhausting his human
strength to defeat the Shadow that
seems to grow larger each passing
year, more and more dread looming
over him.

And then, after a final quantum effort
when he can't pursue his hated life
any longer, his arms splayed outward
in powerless anguish, he collapses
in his own humiliated scream,

crying out in disbelief,
"I am defeated."

Mortified by his self-condemned
weakness, agonizing over his
Shadow's victory
he admits his powerlessness
and surrenders to the unknown.

It is eerily quiet in the liminal space
where he waits … waits for final
judgment and disgrace, waits for
more torture, waits to be devoured,
waits to be cast into hell.

Oddly, in this solitary waiting place,
the feeling of dread slowly leaves him
and something comforting embraces
him, like a loving parent holding a
rebellious child.

In this place of unknowing
where the clear and the nebulous
bow to each other and crystalize,
Light and Shadow tenderly embrace,
whispering smiling silences to each
other, celebrating the soul's
long-awaited union.

As Light illuminates the Shadow,
the Shadow fades as if it never existed.
A weight is lifted, only peace remains.
Confusion, anger, frustration are gone.
He feels like dancing, laughing, loving.

Then suddenly, the floor disappears.
He falls through a mist.
As the view clears, he is standing,
holding a rock in his hand, angry at
someone who is cowering in a corner.

As the man raises his arm to throw
the rock at the coward, the man's
attention is drawn toward an unusual
fellow, who seems to have a light
around him. He is squatting on the
ground, flashing a loving smile
at the man.

The smile envelopes the man
in indescribable love,
and the man wants to run and hug
and kiss the light-filled fellow,
but something holds the man back.
Looking at the man, the light-filled
fellow glances from the man, to the
cowering one and then back to the man.

The man, filled with love and joy,
drops the rock and runs to the cowering
one, lifts him to his feet, and embraces
the cowering one. As the man
draws back, he sees the face of the
cowering man shift to that of the
light-filled man.

Puzzled, the man turns to the squatting,
light-filled man, who is still squatting
on the ground, lovingly smiling at him.
The man turns and looks into the face
of the cowering one, only to find the face

shift from that of the light-filled man
to that of the man's own face.

His own cowering self's eyes plead
with him, begging him to see himself
and to love himself. But the man is
repelled by the sight of his
weak, helpless self.

The man turns to the squatting,
light-filled fellow in hopes that the
smiling man returns him to that
blissful state of peace and love.
But the light-filled fellow is gone.

The man, now confused and distressed
at having been abandoned by his
light-filled friend, turns back to his
cowering self. Fear overtakes the man
and he prays for help. The light-filled
man is immediately at the man's side,
hugging the man's cowering self.

As the man watches the savior loving
his wounded cowering self, love fills
the man's own chest, and bliss radiates
through him. The man grabs and hugs
his weak, cowering self, and for the first
time in his life, the man cries.

The man's eyes open, and he awakens
from the dream.

The 43 Year Flood

The river was still
on the Meramec that night.
We were camped on the bank
not knowing the blight.

Clouds gathered quickly,
rain pelted the fire,
we huddled in tents
not knowing it was dire.

Then the dam burst upstream
water flooded the road.
Cut off from escape,
Dad honked a rescue code.

Put the kids in the trees
I heard one of them shout.
The water was up to the hood
there was no doubt.

The women were panicked
the men like at war
praying to escape
the drowning not far.

Two boats came afloat
the decision was done
children-mothers, different boats
but I was told I'd have fun.

The woman hugged me tight
her fear I could feel
but she smiled and said
this is fun—no big deal.

I wanted my mom
I was four—just a child,
We were going to perish
My fear was so wild.

But I was told this was fun
so my terror I swallowed
I became her brave dear
and doubted my sorrow.

Forty-three years later
the flood raged inside me.
When I sought fun
the panic gushed around me.

It had drowned me each day
since that event long ago
linking fun and danger
it had jaded me so.

The flood inside has subsided
I will not drown
I have found peace of mind
I stand on firm ground.

The Stallion and the Eagle

Hoofs thundering and pounding softened earth,
splitting and spewing pellets of mud and
flashing masses of water into the air after a recent rain.

The stallion's nostrils flare for air as he forces his muscles,
straining and bulging, to move him forward,
galloping against the breeze,
stirring winds circling his aliveness,
his mane and tail flagging in the wind.

He slows to a stop, shaking off sweat.
He rears with his freedom—whinnying his exhilaration.
His strength and power are testimony
of the earthen part of him upon which he runs.

The breeze whistles through the eagle's feathers,
a slight, almost silently, mystical rhythm
declaring the eagle's existence,
as he glides quietly, circling, diving, floating.

His only affirmation for the earth
is his shadow dancing and swirling
on the grass and mud below him.
He perches as gently as a canary onto a branch,
and then, spreading his wings,
he falls like a well-aimed arrow, wings back,
commanding the wind to carry him
swiftly and elegantly.
His grace and sureness are testimony
of the infinite part of him in which he flies.

The strength and power of the stallion
rouse the earthen in me,
and the grace and sureness of the eagle
proclaim the ethereal in me—
Together lies my freedom and my identity.

The Light That Beckons

The Light over the manger of times old
Beckoned within each a seed to unfold

The Light called all who held it dear
So long ago, in a night so clear

But that Bible story happened long ago
There is no light now, or it's very low

In everyone, the Light flickers—waits to erupt
Everyone equal, from peacemaker to corrupt

The wondrous Light of Love calls Its own
Blessing all those who wish to come Home

The darkness blinds you—you feel alone
You will see clearly, it is you you disown

And when, like the flower, the seed is ready
The Light explodes within, strong and steady

The earth cracks from pole to pole
Shaking those who seek to be whole

Into their abyss floods this luminous Light
That offers them sanctuary from their plight

The Light calls Itself in each to be
The Light of the world for all to see

The Maker and the Made

Today, we visited our new church organ,
It was in pieces everywhere ... pipes, keys and wood.
Each and every piece made by human hands.
It was like an unborn child, in the midst of being created.

The organ maker told us about the organ, and then ...
He made a pipe for us,
A simple tube, but oh, how unique and exquisite.
Being born with its own sound, its own calling.

But during this pipe's creation,
it was the organ maker I watched—not the pipe.
For in seeing him, I saw the ecstasy
that God experiences when creating.
As the man worked, it was as if he became the pipe itself.

He touched it, molded it, and studied it.
His fingers were gentle, caressing it as he carefully
measured, glued, filed. And he lovingly
bent over it in his toil, making sure it was perfect.

He was just a person when he spoke to us about the organ,
But when he touched the pieces he created,
he became transfigured. It was as if his soul awoke,
and sprang forth with gladness at loving and being loved,
moving him beyond the manual task
to the heart of hearts where his calling dwelled.

And in the finished pipe and the man's contented soul,
I could feel God's love surround both
the maker and the made,
both lifted up, blessed and cherished.

We are all the Maker and the Made.
In seeking our Calling,
we allow God to create through us
as we create ourselves.

We claim our divine essence by surrendering
to God's creative hand and are inspired to create
the magic that God weaved
into us to bring forth His Beauty.

Let us not be afraid to give ourselves
over to the Divine Maker
to be Made in God's image,
for it is in the offering of our souls
to the Benevolent One that we are made whole.

The Mother Harpist

We are strings upon which the Mother Harpist
places her delicate fingers
and as She plucks our individual string,
we begin to vibrate with resonance.
We have within us the tone that we sing,
but alone we are mute and lifeless.
It is the Harpist, whose song is in Her fingertips,
who blesses our gift of expression.

We pour forth our melody onto the wind,
and our notes float across the airs.
The rhythm of our own string
blends with the other strings that are plucked,
making our tone even more harmonious and sweet,
as together we fill the ethers with symphonic declaration.

The Harpist is intimate with each string,
and takes special care to honor its offering
that expresses Her Song over the earth.

Our human mother's hands touching us
are our joy and our agony.
Her touch is the expression of her surrender
to the Harpist's touch.
As children we know we are loved
by the warmth that erupts in our heart
when our mother touches us with joy.

But when at times our mother's song is mournful,
we children long to bring her touch into harmony
with the Mother Harpist.
But how can we? The stream cannot direct
the river from which it flows.

We are incomplete
without our mother's loving communion—
our song remains half sung
and echoing within our own heart,
aching to be consummated.

It is only the Harpist who can consummate our wholeness.
If our loving child-heart can offer to the Mother Harpist
our human mother's off-key string for sanctification,
who is then sanctified? Whose song is made whole?

When the Christ in us can love another
in spite of their coarseness,
and we surrender that person in love
over to the Harpist's care,
is it not our own song that is blessed
by the Benevolent Virtuoso?

And, oh, how preciously our uplifted song
fills the ethers as our strings quiver
in melodic perfection orchestrating
Life's sweet and majestic anthem of Love.

The Power of a Nurse

This terror occurs inside my head
Lying here helpless in this bed
I have a fear I will soon be dead.

Nurse, I know you have no time to spare
But my soul is aching and feels such scare
It's almost too much for me to bear.

I've been in this chaos for quite a while
I must act fine, though … that's my style
I'm afraid a tear will betray my smile.

I'm a strong person, but I can't speak
One tear escapes my eye, I feel so weak
You take a tissue and wipe my cheek.

Without saying a word, you really heard
Something inside me is truly stirred
It's just not vision that is now blurred.

I must be stoic and be controlled
The words in my throat remain untold
My soul cries take my hand and hold.

I am silent in pleading my soul's beseech
But then like a cosmic psychic breach
Your hand toward mine it does reach.

Your hand squeezes mine, holds it tight
My inward chaos takes quick flight
Your broad smile is a wonderful sight.

Your empathy shines, you are the chief
You are the one who dissolves my grief
I am grateful to you for such relief.

You release my hand, give me a sign
That everything will be just fine
And peace of mind will be all mine.

Your nursing me was wordless, unsaid
But I feel so full and so very fed
I am less scared, I see health ahead.

Then for the first time, you speak … so clear
"Please rest and relax, you have nothing to fear
We are with you always, be of good cheer."

Out of the Dark

1619 was the year
our lesson did surely start
and from then until this very day
it has torn us apart.

Twenty Africans kidnapped to here
to begin the white man's labor
In 240 years, it would pit
neighbor against neighbor.

The southern whites did the math
an easy way to make a buck
they bought and chained many souls
whites created their own bad luck.

They did not realize what they did
to treat humans as property
this went against God's very laws
to live in such snobbery.

Wrapped in slavery's shroud
for power and for cash
they became an evil demon
insidious with the lash.

They were unconscious of its call
unconscious of its power
and it drew them in hastily
and over them it did tower.

Something broke deep inside
their minds and hearts one day
they trampled the spirit of the Lord
they denied harm in every way.

Each year that evil festered
our nation found it harder to bear
it became so hideously huge
but to view it they did not dare.

It took a life on of its own
it was terrible to see
torn black humans everywhere
a crime our nation couldn't flee.

A war was fought, Blue and Gray
all bleeding unconscious blood
not realizing the victory sought
left their souls behind in the mud.

The Blue fought for the nation
and the blacks' unbearable plight
Gray fought for slavery and state.
Neither one was really right.

The whites up north were no better
with their righteous indignation
they wanted to surely set blacks free
but not give them a foundation.

The war was won, the blacks freed
now life could continue on
but the peoples' diseased hearts
destroyed the peace, it was gone.

The Klan raised up its ugly head
clinging to their hate and rage
but these white men were imprisoned
in their own emotional cage.

Both north and south raised their kids
to view blacks as a threat
the kids soaked up the venom well
they vouched to never forget.

Fear can make us do some things
that we never would otherwise do
it strips us of our loving self
we betray ourselves and are untrue.

Ninety more years slithered along
the nation suppressed by racism
prejudice, violence, bigotry yes
creating an enormous schism.

Then Dr. King came along
a hero if there ever was any
his peaceful words gathered hearts
and freed the minds of many.

His words were soothing to everyone
who wanted to love and not fight
he gathered blacks and whites alike
to walk boldly with God into the Light.

We still have discomfort within our souls
we know it not, but we are shackled
unconscious hate and fear reign within.
Will we find the courage to tackle?

So sixty years more and here we are
some leaders are still booming
fomenting crowds to get their own way
to keep the blacks subhuman.

Four hundred years of cry and pain
misconduct gone badly array
when will we renounce white privilege
and invite Love to rule the day?

To invite love in is to bless ourselves
with redemption, salvation and worth
transform ourselves by renewing our mind
and we give ourselves spiritual birth.

It is time, right now, this very day
to learn the lesson in our heart
when we love and forgive like Christ
celestial joy and peace will start.

The Power of "I Am"

When I say, "I am tired" –
I forfeit my energy.

When I say, "I am enthusiastic" –
I charge myself with zeal.

When I say, "I am poor" –
I desert my abundance.

When I say, "I am prosperous" –
I claim abundance.

When I say, "I am discouraged" –
I refute faith.

When I say, "I am uplifted" –
I acknowledge Spirit in action.

When I say, "I am fearful" –
I victimize myself.

When I say, "I am love" –
I bless the world.

When I say, "I am angry" –
I hide away.

When I say, "I am happy" –
I open myself to joy.

When I say, "I am lonely" –
I despair in separation.

When I say, "I am connected" –
I embrace my relationships.

Standing in Truth, I move from fear to faith

Today I choose who "I AM."

The Soaring of Powerful Eagle

I lie on the grass and watch you—
sometimes you float playfully,
allowing the currents to strum
through your feathers,
and sometimes seriously,
when you dive with full force.

Where are you now, Powerful Eagle?
You have flown beyond my sight
and I fear you will not return.
Are you soaring toward the
Horizon of the Greater Tomorrow,
or seeking refuge for a stilled
journey of an inner quest?

I know your heart is with the Wind
which raises you on high,
and that you will follow the Wind
wherever It carries you,
for you love the Wind
which lifts you up.

And the Wind's voice rises from
the hills and plains rejoicing to hear
your heartbeat in the Secret Places
where you fly together, and in celebration of
your obedience to Its call.

Though you were wounded by an
earth bullet, the Warm Wind embraced
you as an incubating nested egg, as when
you were new. And the Gentle Breeze
healed your wound and lifted you up
on high, proclaiming your magnificence.

What has the Wind to teach you,
Powerful Eagle? And what do you
have to teach me when you return?
What have I to learn
from your absence?

Is it that I need to quiet my wrestling ego—
to surrender my own direction to the lifting
of the Wind's direction—
to offer my own wound to be enfolded
within the Warm Wind—
to allow the Wind to lift me to the highest heights
simply because the Wind loves to share
its Celestial Joy with me?

Or perhaps that time and mortality
are but illusions, which are as
unfettered as the Wind itself; that the
passage of time and mortality are merely
a memory of hazy glaze, which the Wind,
in its mercy, withholds from me until
I am ready to see my divine purpose.

My heart aches that I cannot
see the entire sky, as I lie on the grass
pondering the Wind and your intimacy.

I sense a powerful eagle inside myself.
How could it not be, since I recognize
it in you. You are just a mirror of my Being.
I long to wing with God through the
Universe, stirring others' hearts as
I kiss their souls and give them peace,
like you do to me.

The Violin

A novice playing a violin may make a sound
like that of a screeching chicken being strangled.

A virtuoso playing may make a sound
like that of God's song floating in the breeze.

Does the music come from the violin or the player?

Today, I offer myself up to God
so He may play me as His violin
to express divine love on the breeze.

The Way of It

You believe that your greatest sin
is when you fail—it causes chagrin
Your greatest sin is resisting the dove
That brings God's very precious love

We see God when the sun does rise
Flowers, green grass, and blue skies
We know that God fills the earth
His beautiful gift for our mirth

But what of us, we seem unsure
Has God left us, He seems obscure
We seem to suffer a deep soul pain
Were we branded with a stain?

Our confusion pushes God away
Not wanting judgment—we keep Him at bay
We do this out of guilt, shame and fear
Avoiding damnation, we don't let Him near

We really don't know who we are
That ignorance has left a scar
We huddle and stay very afraid
Pleading with God, we try to persuade

I'm being good, God, please just look
I work hard, and read the Good Book
It tells me, in You I should trust
I'm afraid to, but I know I must

Sweet child, God says with a smile
Don't you know I made you worthwhile
There is nothing of you that is required
Please stop resisting, aren't you tired?

My wish is to love you, not to destroy
It is my great pleasure to give you joy
There is nothing that you have to pay
I gave you free will, you can go or stay

Don't consider yourself a poor little minion
On the contrary, I have given you dominion
You disown yourself when you beg and cower
Stand up straight and claim your power

You ask me to forgive you, you have it wrong
You are my beloved, in my heaven you belong
I made you from Me, you are My expression
We are one and the same, I see no transgression

You are energy like Me, you are not form
After you die, your spirit is still warm
There is nothing to fear, everything is vibration
Transforming fear to love will bring liberation

Acting in fear you may have hurt your mother
Or perhaps your spouse, sister or brother
Forgive yourself and make amend
Do as I do, and love your friend

Your mindset of lack makes you keep taking
You'll know prosperity is yours upon waking
I've imbued you with the essence of giving
When you enact that, you will start living

Rejoice in My love, and you will shine Light
Bring joy to others, it will ease their fright
Ecstasy will whisper from within your soul
Saying I love you, My Child, you are whole

So shine your light brightly for others to see
Seek the Truth and Love will set you free
Life includes joy and lessons to embrace
Open your arms wide and receive God's grace

Those Who Love Selflessly

There are those who toil selflessly
Striving for other people's welfare
Sometimes for many years indeed
Hoping for themselves, they will care.

And what of life's struggles, the pain others feel
You watch as they struggle against odds
One step forward, two steps back
You offer to walk by them and plod.

For those who choose this high mission
Praying for those lost, wounded and falling
It can be frustrating and tiring at times
Can't they feel your love, know your calling?

But you seek the words and the wisdom
To help these fellow travelers stand tall
You wonder is it worth it? What will it bear?
Have faith. Providence is orchestrating the call.

Your mission is to walk the path
Your own life being the example
Finding yourself, opening to love
That is all you can do; it is ample.

Then a smile appears on their exhausted face
Their fist unclenches, their hand it does reach
And you take their hand, and you smile too
As joy fills the hearts of each.

And think how much more God is smiling
When you yourself listened and sought
For that person is only a mirror, you see,
You called out and look what God brought.

For those of you who never give up
Bringing love, hope and peace to each scene
You are a blessing indeed to everyone
Because your love touches everything.

We Are All Teachers

For all the teachers in our lives
who have cared, guided and blessed us
with their presence and wisdom,
let us thank them.

We are all teachers.
We teach best by example
and by the way we live our lives.
Some of us are examples of
how NOT to do something,
and those people can be as valuable
as the positive role models in our lives.

Teaching can be as simple as a smile.
If a person is in despair,
a simple smile conveys a message of hope.
That smile may change their life.

Never underestimate how we can teach.

When All Else Fails

When all else fails, surrender to love.

Your Prayer Creates Your Life

Is this your prayer? I am broken and hopeless.

or

Is this your prayer? I am whole and grateful.

Be aware of how you pray.
It will slave you or it will save you.

Centering Prayer

Centering Prayer
is my inner manger
where I birth and cherish
my Christ Being.

Faith is Believing and Knowing

Faith is believing and knowing
that a Higher Power will light
your way as you enter the
darkest tunnels of your life.

Castles in the Air

Dreamers build castles in the air
and wait endlessly to win at the fair
They always seem to be on guard
Maneuvering for a great reward

They'll still be waiting in their grave
Never quenching the thirst they crave
Their life itself seems so unstable
Chasing after a traditional fable

Pray-ers seem to build castles afar
As if reaching for a twinkling star
What's the difference, do you know?
One seeks a foe, the other a flow

The dreamer sacrifices his soul
For that illusive title role
The pray-er, on the other hand,
Gets still and seeks what is planned

The dreamer constantly runs amuck
Chasing the almighty buck
The pray-er seeks solace inside
Listening for the inner Guide

It takes faith for the pray-er to open wide
To let go of their ego pride
Sitting in the silent place
They still their mind, they stop the race

Letting wisdom slowly come to them
Seeking only to touch the healing hem
They seek their answer in the quiet
Not in mindless chatter that erupts riot

Dreamers and pray-ers, at a glance,
Both seem to be in a dream-like trance
But the dreamer has no firm foundation
That will power his imagination

The pray-er has a secret power
The very thing that grows a flower
You can't see it, it has no bound
Only in the quiet can it be found

The dreamer seeks to be the victor
Success for him, that is the predictor
To stomp a competitor to the ground
And seek the glory, to be crowned

There are no "ifs" for a true pray-er
In his world there is no betrayer
He seeks to only open his soul
To realize that he's already whole

God uses a tender touch to prep
Lays out the plan step by step
Spirit always has a mission
But the pray-er does not seek ambition

That's the difference between the two
Dreamer and pray-er, most never knew
Ambitious King David, he would kill
Where Jesus Christ would love and fulfill

We are the dreamer, we are the pray-er
Within us, we must work through each layer
It only takes a choice, a vision
To change our life with one decision

We change by shifting what is dear
When love is the quest there is no fear
But for those who seek the material form
There's suffering and an inward storm

Instead of crazily moving fast
Let's just stop, let go, and ask
What is it You wish me to do today?
And Love will guide you on your way

You may sit at the well and wait a while
And your heart of hearts will soon smile
As you are led to a despairing dreamer
And through your love he will find the Redeemer

Knowing the Absolute Truth

Knowing the Absolute Truth,
that Spirit is Changeless Law,
Love and Harmony, becomes a compass
that leads us to our Freedom.

Stepping Into the Waters of Life

Then Jesus stepped into the water and approached John.
As John placed his hands on Jesus,
God's Grace and Blessing descended and surrounded Jesus,
and peace welled up in both of their hearts.
Thus began Jesus's ministry.

Each day as you step into the water of life,
may God's Grace and Blessing surround you,
and may you and the people you touch
be filled with God's peace.

Spirit Provides Our Need

Spirit provides our need, step by step.
It does not place obstacles on the path.
Our unbelief is what blocks our way.

A Limerick About Job (from the Bible)

There once was a man named Job
Who God favored with a bright strobe
Job worshipped God as divine
And his life was quite fine
God blessed him with life's best robe

Job's loyalty was questioned by Satan
Who wagered God that Job would unstraighten
Job's faith he'd lose quick
If he should get sick
Job would curse God loudly and blatant

God thought that Job was a good guy
And God knew he'd win, easy as pie
Satan could make Job suffer
But Job would stay tougher
Job would not betray God or ask why

Satan zapped Job's family and they died
And Job, heartbroken, sat and cried
Body covered with sores
Other troubles by the score
Job was trying to take this torment in stride

Job talked with three of his friends
Who told him his actions must offend
Job must have done wrong
But Job would not play along
He claimed his innocence all the way to the end

Job was quite confused, angry and bitter
He asked God, "Are you a counterfeiter?"
Demanding God answer he must

I've been good, why are you unjust
Job's emotions almost made him a quitter

God appeared to Job as a whirlwind
Showing Job wherein he had sinned
God's world was too amazing
For Job's thinking to be appraising
God invited Job to trust, not be chagrined

God honored Job's honesty and prayer
Job prevailed over the pain he did bear
He faced toward God's light
Understood at a new height
Realizing that life was a complex affair

Job's faith caused him to kneel and repent
He was thankful that God let him vent
Job spoke rightly of the Lord
Never did fall overboard
God restored Job's treasures, with happy intent

The morale of the story is this
Listen well or the answer you'll miss
You can't see the big picture
Because of ego stricture
So trust in God and find true bliss

God's world is an amazing place
It is brimming with divine holy grace
But suffering occurs too
To be faced by hearts true
So believe, love and trust God's embrace

The Oasis

The soles of my bare feet sizzle
from the heat of the cracked,
charred desert floor.

My nose dry, my throat parched
from quenchless striving,
I continue trudging forward
searching for sanctuary.

Do I see an oasis ahead?
Could it be real
or just another confusing mirage
and tangle of folly that torments me
in my quest to find nourishment?

I cautiously approach its mysterious entrance.
Surprisingly, the coolness
of a rainbow-colored garden welcomes me.
I feel the moistness of the cool earth
under my feet and smell the garden's fragrance
filling my nose and throat.

The shock from barren to plenty engulfs me,
and a surge of hope enlivens my soul.

I lie in the cool grass and melt into nature's arms
and I pray this is real and true.

And as sleep draws nigh,
a bird's comforting lullaby bids me rest.

Circle of Life

To love is to let go
To let go is to accept
To have faith is to know God
To know God is to realize Selfhood
To realize Selfhood is to love
To love is to let go …

Love is Like the Dazzling Sun

Love is like the dazzling sun,
Hot, constant, giving vision

Powerful, giving ... and fun,
Each smile or touch and it's begun

Every warm ray an infusion
Get still, receive, let love quietly run

Love will bless you until the day is done!
You are loved!

Prodigal

It came to pass that the young man,
disgusted with himself and
filled with self-loathing,
had burnt his bridges and
had nowhere else to go
but to return to his father's home.

Broke and starving, he stumbled along,
lashing himself with his own embarrassment
and self-hatred, ready to beg
for his father's lowest and least regard.
What if his father rejected his plea?
Where could he go? He would surely die.

And it came to pass that the father
loved the son very much,
and he had been sad from the day
his son had left.
Each day the father prayed
for the son to return.
Every day he waited …
watched … hoped.

And then one day …
one glorious light-filled day …
far off in the distance
the father saw someone on the path.
Could it be his son?
His heart jumped in his chest.
The person was so thin, walking slowly
with his head down and his shoulders bent.

The father couldn't tell …
but, oh, how he hoped.

The father took a few steps
closer to see clearer.
As the father strained his eyes to see,
the person stopped and began kicking
at the rocks in a pensive way ...
and the father's eyes widened
and a scream of joy leapt from his throat—
his son would kick rocks like that
when he was troubled. His son had come home!

The father ran to his son,
waving his arms and bounding with glee.
The son, seeing his father running
wildly toward him, stepped back in surprise.
The father flung his arms
around his son's dirty, stinking body,
kissing him repeatedly.

The father ordered his servants afoot
and a feast was prepared.
And the father refused to hear the
son's groveling pleas of unworthiness.
His beautiful son was back home,
and the old man's heart
was overflowing with blessings.

It is not what we do
but what we Are that God celebrates ...
    be not afraid ...
        Come Home.

Three Little Words

Three little words that are preferred
That are not spoken enough or heard
Three little words that are so true
Will quickly chase away the blues
Say them clearly, say it often
And the world's heart will soften
Three little words that are always new
Tell someone today, "I love you!"

Throwing Stones

And then as He drew in the dirt,
all the while affirming love
for the angry mob and the terrified woman,
one by one each condemning person
dropped their stone and left the woman,
until there was no one there to harm her.

Today, as we walk through our day
let us affirm the highest thought of love
for ourselves when we condemn others and
for others when they condemn us.

As we cast love instead of stones,
we ascend in consciousness, joy and peace.

Father's Day

Father's Day is to celebrate dads
who provide safety to help us explore
and who teach us strength to find our way Home.

Every day Divine Masculine celebrates Father's Day
by creating an inner sanctuary of personal safety
that allows an outer freedom to express without fear.

Every day Divine Masculine celebrates Father's Day
by engaging the strength to love in spite of injustice
and offering an outstretched hand to help overcome.

Today—Father's Day—I witnessed Divine Masculine
create a sacred place of safety and strength
within the Holiest of Holies.

In this place, which invited expression of depth,
one of the wounded touched her pain
that was caused by an injustice she had endured.

From the others came a beam of Love
to help her feel safe and accept,
and their outstretched hands helped her find Home.

When they uplifted her expressed pain,
there came an overpowering Oneness,
lifting all of them to their Divinity.

A visionary congregation of people,
spiritual beacons illuminating the world,
blessing all who cross their path.

And as they left and entered into their day,
their hearts in love were still connected
to each other and to Abba, the Father who blesses them.

Wisdom

A three year old child
sits in the sandbox
feeling the breeze
kiss his cheek
as he fills his bucket
with sand.

He hears the
swaying treetop whisper,
"Wissssss-dom, wis-doooom."
The sand he pours
whispers "wiss-dom."
The faster he pours
the louder the sand
reveals itself, "WISDOM."

The sun winks at him
through clouds, "wisdom."
His heart shouts "Wisdom."
The plants and stones shout "wisdom"
as he runs by them toward his mother.

With his epiphany
beaming out of his celestial face,
he laughs and falls
into his mother's arms.
She hugs him,
"Billy, my wise, loving boy."
He laughs as he climbs into her lap,
knowing he already shelters
wisdom's sacred secret in his heart.

"You gambled our house away!
Lady Luck is a whore, Bill!
She promises everything
and then leaves you … us …
with nothing!
You're 30 years old.
When are you going to WAKE UP?"
his wife screams as she drives away
for the last time.

He walks aimlessly,
mumbling to himself,
mesmerized by his mortified agony.
"We were so happy. I worked so hard—
then, poof, like the wind, it was gone.
What's the meaning of it all?
What have I got to live for?"

A child's laughter shakes him
from his misery.
He sees a jubilant little boy
fall into his mother's arms.
The treetops above sway
with a long-ago sound.
An ancient sense of completeness
stirs in him, and for a moment,
peace flitters in his heart,
then agony again.

The old man sits alone reflecting on his life.
"By the grace of God,
I have not gambled in 40 years.
I thank you for that, God,
but why heart disease AND cancer?
I've built my life up from nothing.
Helped so many people rebuild their lives.

I'm a good person.
Why are these bad things happening to me?
Did I do something to deserve this?"

Bill closes his eyes and waits for an answer:
Through a foggy muffle, he hears a woman calling him.
Far off, he hears a child laughing—
then realizes he is the child who is laughing.
He is three, shoveling sand—
the sand is saying something.
The trees seem to talk to him,
the breeze is whispering, too,
the sun is winking a secret at him.
He can't quite hear their message?

The woman's call beckons him—
suddenly the childhood sacred secret
bursts from his heart.
He is on his feet, running—
he IS the ground, the air, the sand,
the breeze, the tree, the sun, the butterfly,
his mother's smile. As he falls into
Divine Feminine's embrace,
the voice whispers,
   "You are one Blessed Breath
      in the ethers from which
        all Synergy flows.
          You know this as a child,
            but not as a man.
              Continue to trust my wisdom,
                my Holy Son."

With this, Bill is wide-eyed awake.
Tears of joyous clarity
and utter confusion
pour from his eyes.

In the midst of
not knowing, he knows,
and in the midst of
knowing, he knows nothing.

He lowers his head to Wisdom's sacred paradox.
As he sanctifies his faith and acceptance
with tearful gracious gratitude,
Wisdom welcomes him Home.

The Miracle

When I was young, I met a man
in a college cafeteria, of all places, offhand
he was a charmer, a liar, a sneak, and a cheat
I liked him despite this, so glad we did meet

Alcohol was his savior and his buddy.
when he drank, his mind became muddy
but as my friend drank his fill
I watched as Drink began to kill

Downing the gimlets—witty, charming and bold
our friendship and laughter hid what was untold
that my friend would die, if truth be told
in this merciless battle so very cold

I prayed that my friend wouldn't be beat
that he would work through it and land on his feet
but, on my friend, Drink did take its toll
I was afraid my friend might never be whole

While Drink patted his back, it was stealing his soul
it would be curtains unless he faced this demon's hold
alcoholism raised its fist for a final blow
its message was clear—death was its goal

My friend began hemorrhaging, a bender gone bad
knew that Drink had tricked him—he had been had
he went to AA, walked the talk and was glad
he stayed sober, free from going mad

I watched him change, get honest and clean,
into a wise man, with character serene
sharing his experience, strength and hope
helping others face their life and cope

I thank friends, fellowship, and, of course, God
working through meetings and his AA squad,
for sharing always the message of love,
so we all can live freely below and above.

Made in the USA
Monee, IL
13 August 2021

74799024R00066